THE RIVER *of* HOPE

DAVID HAAS

THE RIVER *of* HOPE

A VISION OF FAITH AND MINISTRY

A Crossroad Book
The Crossroad Publishing Company
New York

The Crossroad Publishing Company
370 Lexington Avenue, New York, NY 10017

Printed in the United States of America

Library of Congress Cataloging-in-Publication Data

Haas, David.
The river of hope : a vision of faith and ministry / by David Haas.
p. cm.
ISBN 0-8245-1740-7 (pbk.)
1. Hope – Religious aspects – Christianity. I. Title.
BV4638.H22 1999
234′.25–dc21 98-35065

1 2 3 4 5 6 7 8 9 10 03 02 01 00 99

In memory of
Madelin Sue Martin,
mentor,
light,
hopeful servant

Wherever the river goes,
every living creature that swarms will live,
and there will be very many fish,
once these waters reach there.
It will become fresh;
and everything will live where the river goes.

—Ezekiel 47:9

Contents

Foreword

For me the words of Ezekiel, "Everything will live where the river flows," are worth the price of this book. In these pages my friend David draws us into currents of hope. He knows that hope is a dynamic bigger and stronger than intellectual concept or will power. Hope catches us. Hope flows through us. Maybe it's because David is a singing man that he writes about hope as a river. When he sings, he is a man caught up, a man in flow. When he sings, he becomes the song he is singing. And his singing makes him brave. In these pages he speaks the truth as he sees it, not looking over his shoulder for approval or disapproval.

There's refreshing truth in this little book. It washes over you like a stream. It is filled with the Spirit of Jesus. I invite you to embark on these waters and to let them carry you. And I hope that from these pages you'll flow over into David's music — hearing it and singing it. Whenever I sing his songs, hope flows through me and makes me brave. David has given us the gift of himself in these pages.

Sister Helen Prejean, CSJ

River of Hope

River,
deep river,
moving,
pushing.

Slow at first,
my life preserver fastened tightly—
"steady as she goes,"
with serenity and stillness
in my sight.
Open sailing.

You provide
interesting turns;

my arms stiffening,
surprised,
unexpecting,
the current is off course.
Only my feet are grounded—
welded to the wood floor,
relentless.

River,
I see land in sight,
but there are diversions and rocks;
the water is thicker,
and the bottom blurred.
More algae than earth,
more mud than sand,
greener,
with a scent that I did not
bargain on.

No turning back,
many are watching
—the birds and creatures are singing to me now—

having a better view than I,
knowing the way
and having observed others
before me.
They chuckle lightly,
but for me all the way,
at the same time
leaving me to my own devices.

Your rings that circle 'round
form a shaky movement
and take my boat
and the oars into a tug-of-war
between the forces of your path
and the will of my spirit.

Your moist voice
pilots my journey,
keeping me on course
—though not knowing
or believing at the time—
continuously faithful.

The River of Hope

I surrender to you,
yet still fearful,
wondering why I'm here.

Watching is more fun
than participating;
certainly easier,
certainly safer,
and certainly
the heart beats more readily,
the breathing seems more steady,
back and forth,
back and forth,
like a mantra.

Your voice still needles me,
leading me
to land where I would
rather not go.
Please — not now.
For its flaws are many,
the ground is soft,

River, I realize you are the only way possible.

the trees are weak,
and bearing fruits that are
perhaps poisoned,
or tainted with a taste
that I have not yet acquired.

River, I realize
you are the only way possible.

I fear you,
yet you are my friend.

I wonder if I can depend
on your road map
which is never predictable,
never reliable,
never routine,
never directed toward
a place
that is familiar to me,
but interesting nonetheless.
Very interesting.

Keep moving, River,
flow and carry me.
I hate treading water;
encourage me
to ride the wave:
"Let go,
stop resisting."
Lead me to

dry ground,
a place to once again
watch and learn.
"Dance to my tempo."

Without you, I stay docked
and never discover
the waves and currents
where you live.
The invitation is there.
A new Eden,
a garden of colors that is watered
by your rhythm,
by your music;
anchored by your unique language
that, while not always
easy to understand,
speaks the truth.

I am lowering the lifeboats,
holding my breath—
here we go!

One

Making the Case for Hope

For surely I know the plans I have for you,
says the Lord,
plans for your welfare and not for harm,
to give you a future with hope.

—JEREMIAH 29:11

Making the Case for Hope

WHENEVER CHRISTIANS GATHER TOGETHER,
we do so in hope.
We come to offer ourselves in worship and service
not because we want to have a good time
or because we are in need of escape,
but because of our commitment and confession
that Jesus Christ is the Lord of our lives.
Hope is at the center of our faith;
hope is what keeps us moving forward
when we feel paralyzed;
hope is the song that we keep singing
when it seems that all sanity
has abandoned our world.
We cling to this world by our fingernails sometimes,
and the story of hope at these times
gives us the foundation and footing

that keeps us from freefall.
The metaphor and image of "God Is Love"
is experienced in faith as "God Is Hope."
The hope of God's creation
proclaimed in the Hebrew Scriptures
is the hope that the world is good
and that God is in charge.

As followers of Christ we believe that
he is the completion of that promise of hope.
But honestly, who is Christ?
It is the question that Jesus asks his disciples
and asks of us:
"Who do people say that I am?"
Many answers come forward from those
who originally followed in faith,
and of course many of us
have taken the journey to answer this question
on the basis of our own experience
as well as on the basis of our study
of theology and spirituality.
But more directly, Jesus asks:

"Who do *you* say that I am?"
Peter answers, "You are the Christ, the Messiah,
the anointed king from the house of David,
expected to come and deliver Israel from its enemies
and establish a world empire,
marked with justice and peace."
Today it might sound like:
"You are the alpha and omega,
the beginning and end,
you are the eschatological promise and eternal logos
which brings meaning, purpose, and clarification
to our existence
and to all of our interpersonal relationships."
I often wonder how Jesus might respond
to such an answer.

Who is Christ?
There have been so many attempts
to answer this question.
But probably the most honest response,
the most faith-filled response,
is the cry of surrender

that Thomas the Apostle models for us
when he is faced with the risen Christ:
"My Lord and my God."
It is in the cry of surrender and obedience,
it is in the practice of listening and reaching out,
that we find the most honest,
the most credible "explanation"
of who this Jesus is,
of what this way of life means for us,
and of what our future holds
if we choose to believe.

The promise of hope is proclaimed and nurtured
in three ways:
in what we believe,
in how we pray,
and in the way we live.

What We Believe

It is difficult to talk about belief
in a time when cynicism and hopelessness

are rampant and pervasive.
Our world in our time is more influenced
by what we know,
by what we can prove, than by belief,
which is perceived as naivete.
Ours is a culture obsessed with the need
for facts and logic
and impatient with the mythic nature of true belief.
And the facts that we are surrounded with
are not encouraging.
They are the facts of a world gone mad,
where war is the solution
in times of conflict,
where selfishness and greed are the basis
for happiness and security,
and where the practice of
trust, love, forgiveness, and compassion
is impossible and not even considered.

The decline in belief
comes with the continuous breakdown
of promises and commitments.

Talk is cheap,
and intentions are not noble any more.

We experience time and time again
that promises are to be broken,
commitments are carelessly abandoned,
and the ability to believe in anything anymore
is critically cheapened.
Broken marriages,
broken promises,
lies from our leaders
in both society and the church,
and the continuous failure of the human condition
makes us jaded and suspicious
of any creed or path of faith.

What we believe is not adequately expressed
simply in the words of the creed
we repeat Sunday after Sunday in our parishes:
"I believe in one Lord Jesus Christ,
the only Son of God,
eternally begotten of the Father,

God from God,
light from light,
true God from true God,
begotten, not made,
one in being with the Father."
While these words are important,
they do not make my faith come alive,
they do not necessarily result
in the complete investment
of the totality of my life.
I do not encounter the Christ
by an exercise of my brain,
but only if I reach out
to the Christ present
in my brothers and sisters.
My faith will have integrity and possibility
only if I love as well as I believe.
It is in my servanthood
that I see and experience
the living face of God,
not in the mere memorization
of a doctrinal formula.

How We Pray

Eucharist is the central and sublime hope
that Christ gave us:
"This is my body, which is given for you."
Ritual and prayer are the way that we Christians
build the strength and muscle that we need
to survive and pound the pilgrim path in our lives.
Ritual has always been
the source of wordless energy for Christians.
Our approach to prayer can be a source
of great angst and frustration
as we struggle to reach true communion with God.
We look for the right spiritual path;
we look for a good spiritual director,
make an annual retreat,
engage in spiritual reading,
or become involved in a prayer group.
We explore many different spiritual practices
such as meditation,
the prayer of examen,
the liturgy of the hours,

"This is my body, which is given for you." (Luke 22:19)

and yet still we often feel dissatisfied,
and we often feel discouraged.
We pray to God for the things we want and need,
and often we say,
"Well, God didn't answer my prayer."
But our faith constantly proclaims
that God always listens and answers our prayers.
The problem is that we often do not like the answer.

God is always answering,
always responding,
but the problem is that we often are not *listening*.
True and honest prayer is less an exercise
in "asking" for something
than a discipline in "listening"
to what God is trying to say,
a true attentiveness to the voice of the Holy.

My primary vocation has been
the ministry of liturgical music.
Music ministers as leaders of sung prayer
have always been called to be heralds of hope.
In the ancient synagogue,
one was chosen to be a cantor
not because of vocal prowess or virtuosity,
but because of the life of integrity
that the person lived in the midst of the community.
The music minister was never a person
who lived in isolation from the community,
but was rather fully invested
in the lives of the people.

Sing aloud,
O daughter Zion;
shout, O Israel!
Rejoice and exult
with all your heart,
O daughter Jerusalem!

(Zeph 3:14)

Their prayer book was the Psalms,
the prayers and the cries of the people.
The Psalter expresses the entire galaxy of emotions
that make up the human condition:
joy, sorrow, pain, ecstasy, loneliness,
despair, anger, rage, hope.

One can proclaim praise and lament
only in relationship with others
and in touch with those realities and dynamics
in one's own life.

This is not a grounding
exclusive to ministers of music;
rather it is for all who minister,
whether in liturgical ministries,
catechetical ministries,
justice ministries,
or ministries of pastoral care.
Our call and charge demand
that we live our life
as ministers with passion
in constant relationship
with those whom we serve.
Are we willing to share
both our joy and our tears?
For myself and other music ministers,
our obsession with our Sunday morning worshipers
is so often "getting the people to sing."
We so often ask the wrong questions
and spend our energies looking at symptoms
rather than the deeper illness.
As a music minister,
I should be asking a profound and difficult question:

What do the people have to sing about?
What do I have to sing about?
Where is my hope?
We sometimes become more concerned
about *what* to sing
than about the more critical question:
Why do we sing?
Are the songs that we sing on Sunday
songs that we can truly believe in?
Music is an incredibly powerful language,
an incredibly prayerful language.
It is one thing to say, "I love you,"
but it is something else again to sing it.
It is one thing to say "Alleluia,"
but it is something different when we sing it.
And if we choose to sing,
it had better ring true.

My life flows on in endless song,
above earth's lamentation.
I hear the real though far-off hymn
that hails a new creation.

Through all the tumult and the strife,
I hear the music ringing.
It sounds and echoes in my soul,
how can I keep from singing?

No storm can shake my inmost calm
while to that rock I'm clinging.
Since love is Lord of heaven and earth,
*how can I keep from singing?**

Our personal prayer life
and our communal liturgical life
need to be reexamined and pursued passionately
if we are to continue to minister in hope.

The Way We Live

The way we live should not be canonical adherence,
a mere conformity to rules and regulations.

---

*"How Can I Keep from Singing?" traditional Quaker hymn, verses 1, 2, and refrain.

There are two basic commandments for our lives,
which shape the need, purpose, and goal of hope:
love God and love your neighbor.
Living with integrity cannot be achieved
simply by reading the new catechism,
but by a true attentiveness to and investment in
the Word of God given to us
in this most simple yet challenging call:
love God and love your neighbor.

In John's Gospel we hear Jesus say:
"Apart from me you can do nothing" (John 15:5).
Without Christ my singing,
my music making,
my entire ministry is a lie,
and without Christ
liturgy becomes an empty ceremony.
Without Christ our programs
and endless meetings in the parish
become hypocrisy of the highest order.
Again, the words of Jesus
penetrate all of my surface concerns:

"Do you love me?"
What do I think Christ means to me?
I try not to think as much as I used to,
but rather to remember how God has loved me,
forgiven me, and walked with me.
When I do that, I do not think so much,
but I do tend to *love* more.

When tyrants tremble sick with fear,
I hear their death knells ringing.
When friends rejoice both far and near,
how can I keep from singing?

No storm can break my inmost calm
while to that rock I'm clinging.
Since love is Lord of heaven and earth,
*how can I keep from singing?**

---

*"How Can I Keep from Singing?" traditional Quaker hymn, verse 3 and refrain.

Two

The Seduction of Hopelessness

My God, my God, why have you forsaken me?
Why are you so far from helping me,
from the words of my groaning?
O my God, I cry by day, but you do not answer;
and by night, but find no rest.

—PSALM 22:1–2

The Seduction of Hopelessness

Despair permeates every space
of our existence:
our personal and collective soul,
our culture,
and even the church.
Broken families and divorce
are the reality in every community;
domestic violence,
abandoned and abused children,
poverty and sickness are rampant.
The million-dollar industry
of Twelve Step recovery and self-help books
reflects the deep realities
of shame, addiction, co-dependency,
chronic depression, and manic hopelessness.
Crime and violence have become

"I was hungry. . . "
(Matt. 25:35)

the overwhelming concern
of the majority of our society;
war and genocide are unchecked;
hunger and homelessness surround us;
and the number of lives lost to AIDS increases
at a rate too fast to fathom.

Racism and discrimination on the basis of
color, belief, gender, and sexual orientation
are profoundly present in every aspect of
cultural, societal, and church life.

Clericalism and domination
in the institutional church
have led to mass discouragement and frustration
for dedicated people in professional ministry
and for volunteers and the folks in our parishes.
There is unbelievable disillusionment
with our church leaders,
thanks to revelations
of sexual abuse and cover-ups
perpetrated by members of the clergy,
resulting in massive lawsuits
and pain and suffering for the victims.
Theologians dedicated to the search for truth
are silenced, shamed, and punished.
Parishes are forced to close
because of the lack of male celibate priests,
and more and more communities
are deprived of Sunday Eucharist.
At the same time
many gifted and qualified women and married men
are told that their gifts are not wanted,
that they do not truly "represent Christ."

These conditions can cripple us,
and the result is a sickness,
a sickness to our very being.
The sickness is insidious
because we are often not even aware of it.
In fact, it is luring, seductive,
and even rewarded in our families,
in our world, and in the church.
We live in a society and church where,
perfectionism, capitalism, nationalism,
consumerism, sexism, racism,
and all the other "isms"
rule and reign over our lives.
The damage is deep
and has often conquered our spirit,
our optimism,
and our belief in the possibility of change
and a better way of living.
To come to terms with the sickness means
first to sit in the muck and mire
and deal with the situation
in which we find ourselves.

I am not a mechanism, an assembly of various sections.
And it is not because the mechanism is working wrongly,
that I am ill.
I am ill because of wounds to the soul, to the deep emotional self
and wounds to the soul take a long, long time, only time can help
and patience, and a certain difficult repentance
long, difficult repentance, realisation of life's mistake, and the freeing oneself
from the endless repetition of the mistake
*which mankind at large has chosen to sanctify.**

Humankind has truly sanctified and enshrined
our hopelessness
and the terminal numbness that paralyzes.

In order to escape from our own fear,
we need to call upon God

---

*D. H. Lawrence, "Healing," from D. H. Lawrence: *Poems Selected and Introduced by Keith Sagar,* rev. ed. (London: Penguin Books, 1986), 216.

to free us from this bondage.
The ancient liturgy gives us the words:
"Kyrie Eleison!"
We cry: "God reigns!"
God reigns above our sinfulness
and our need to make war.
God is above our selfishness and greed,
our individualism and pride.
God reigns and towers
above our violence and our addictions,
our compulsions for possessions, wealth, and power.
God reigns and pulls us through our failings.
God leads us to healing and acceptance.

We will run and not grow weary,
for our God will be our strength,
and we will fly like the eagle;
*we will rise again.**

* "We Will Rise Again," refrain, by David Haas, copyright © David Haas, published by OCP Publications, Portland, Ore.

Three

The Foolishness of Hope

I consider that the sufferings of this present time
are not worth comparing
with the glory about to be revealed to us.
For the creation waits with eager longing
for the revealing of the children of God;
for the creation was subjected to futility,
not of its own will
but by the will of the one who subjected it,
in hope that the creation itself will be set free
from its bondage to decay
and will obtain the freedom
of the glory of the children of God.

We know that the whole creation
has been groaning in labor pains until now;
and not only the creation, but we ourselves,
who have the first fruits of the Spirit,
groan inwardly while we wait for adoption,
the redemption of our bodies.
For in hope we were saved.
Now hope that is seen is not hope.
For who hopes for what is seen?
But if we hope for what we do not see,
we wait for it with patience.

—ROMANS 8:18–25

For those who inflict oppression,
the most feared force is hope.
It is more powerful than any army of might
and the great enemy for those
who want to control our lives and our history.
Dreamers, musicians, artists, dancers, and poets—
they have always been the most feared,
because their language and expression
are difficult to silence.
In many societies the artists are the ones
who have paid the price of being hopeful
with their very lives.
These voices of hope bring about
the events of our salvation and liberation,
events that turn the world upside down,
that move beyond predictability and control.

The River of Hope

In my travels, I encounter people in parish life,
whether ordinary parishioners, volunteers,
or people in ministry,
who feel a hopelessness
with regard to this liberation.
We still believe that the powers that dominate
have ultimate control.
We forget that God governs our lives,
that God governs our history.
In other words
we still believe more in the powers of the world
than we do in the power of God;
we roll over and play dead
and accept the way things are.
When we lose our remembrance of God in history,
we lose hope.
We have to call to mind
the many liberating events of our history,
because they can offer us the new possibility of faith.
When we open history
we see God's wonderful activity,
and when we see the engaging activity of God,

we can respond.
And it is here that we find hope.

We have to muster up the conviction
that we do not have to continue
in the agony and terror
in which we find ourselves.
Hope pulls us beyond this reality;
hope is an inspiration
that transcends the painful realities that surround us.
Often people come to us and say,
"Well, you have to remain hopeful."
And I often think,
"I can't create this feeling of hope;
it isn't real for me.
I have to somehow rise above,
where I am to find hope."
This is where we get ourselves into trouble,
and why hope is often so difficult to find.

Hope is not a nice feeling or pleasant turn of phrase.
Rather, hope is a very concrete movement

in our history;
it is a movement that can create
transformation and conversion.

We often live in two worlds:
impossibility and possibility.
Hope is the movement
from the impossible to the possible.
Many things that happen around us
at one time seemed impossible.
So many of the changes
that have taken place
in our own personal lives,
in the world,
and even in our church
are changes that we could barely have imagined
at another time.
But these changes
did not happen through magic;
rather, they happened
through awakening, dedication,
and the difficult discipline of hope.

The Foolishness of Hope

"The Lord has risen indeed" (Luke 24:34)

When the first witnesses shouted
the news of the resurrection of Jesus,
they were told they were "foolish."
Yet it was this news
that has become the cornerstone of our faith
and the greatest hope
we could ever know.

In terms of our faith,
foolishness is hope never attempted.
But when we believe,
the course of events changes,
is made new, born again,
and again and again.
The "foolishness" of the resurrection
became the hope
which is the foundation of our faith.
The "foolish" songs of the slaves
always expressed the hope
that those who were enslaved
could and should be free.
The "foolishness" of many small actions
of the civil rights movement
embodied a hope
that turned our country upside down.
The "foolishness" of women gathering
in the early part of this century
to seek the vote
launched a movement for equality
that has only just begun.

The "foolishness" of faith and the prayers of hope
have brought down tyrants.

The saints are the "poster children"
of this foolishness.
Foolishness and holiness are first cousins,
born from the same commitment,
born from the same understanding:
that the only life worth living
is the one fully surrendered to the presence of God.
Holiness is more than doing good deeds;
holiness is the daily recognition
that we need God — desperately.

This "foolishness" is found
in many communities of faith
throughout the world.
In my travels,
I have been fortunate to have experienced first hand
the "troublemaking" that they have engaged in.
I have seen the "foolishness" of many small parishes
that have chosen to rise above

their second-class status and threats of closing
to become not only a powerful community
for their own people
but also to reach out to others in evangelization
and witness to their faith.
I have seen the "foolishness"
of many ethnic communities
that have fought to bring dignity and pride
back to their people,
often at the risk of being robbed
of their land, heritage, and identity.
I have seen the ongoing "foolishness"
of poor communities
that have been a witness of true Christian living
and have not only touched the lives of people
within their communities,
but have provided hope for many in our ministry
who are often tempted by cynicism.

Such foolishness is anything but foolishness.
It is hope:
dedicated, passionate, relentless.

Four

Visionaries and Heroes

I will pour out my spirit on all flesh;
your sons and your daughters shall prophesy,
your old . . . shall dream dreams,
and your young . . . shall see visions.

—JOEL 2:28

WHAT IS THE COMMON ELEMENT
in these foolish stories turned into hope?
The gutsy and heroic commitment of visionaries.
Visionaries are those
who not only see the possibility,
but believe that something better actually exists
at the end of the battle.
And then they have to be willing
to swim down the river.
Not everyone can see the river.
Many do not even know that there is one,
and most do not believe
that there is something at the end.

Those who let the river take them must be prepared
to be the victims of ridicule, sabotage,

and, sometimes, even death.
Remember,
the river of hope always leads
from one place to another,
often from certainty to uncertainty,
from home to a strange and unfamiliar land,
from comfort to the messiness of the questionable.
If we truly pay attention to history,
we see that the common thread of this movement
is that we cannot experience
transformation,
conversion,
and liberation
without cost.
It is never easy;
it is never without pain and suffering.
To speak out is to pay a price,
which is why there are few heroes.

The Scriptures confront us:
"Bringing offerings is futile;
incense is an abomination to me. . . .

Learn to do good;
seek justice,
rescue the oppressed,
defend the orphan,
plead for the widow" (Isa. 1:13, 17).
According to the Letter of James:
"What good is it, my brothers and sisters,
if you say you have faith but do not have works?
Can faith save you?
If a brother or sister is naked and lacks daily food,
and one of you says to them,
'Go in peace; keep warm and eat your fill,'
and yet you do not supply their bodily needs,
what is the good of that?
So faith by itself,
if it has no works,
is dead" (James 2:14–17).
The prophet Micah says:
"What does the Lord require of you,
but to do justice,
and to love kindness,
and to walk humbly with your God?" (Mic. 6:8).

And the blast from the prophet Amos
is indeed fearful for ministers of music like myself:
"I hate, I despise your festivals,
and take no delight in your solemn assemblies. . . .
Take away from me the noise of your songs;
I will not listen to the melody of your harps.
But let justice
roll down like waters,
and righteousness
like an ever-flowing stream" (Amos 5:21, 23–24).

This call to be visionaries of justice
is not an optional offshoot of Christianity
or a nice extracurricular activity
when we have spare time.
Speaking out and creating justice
is the very call of our baptism,
and Jesus began his ministry
with the recognition of his charge:
"The Spirit of the Lord is upon me,
because he has anointed me
to bring good news to the poor, . . .

sent me to proclaim release
to the captives" (Luke 4:18).
We struggle for justice for the poor and oppressed
not because it is compassionate to do so,
but because justice is the gift
that God has chosen to give us.
In the liturgy every Sunday we repeat the words,
"This is my body given for you...
this is the cup of my blood,
the blood of the new and everlasting covenant."
Because we have experienced this love,
we are charged to live
the second great commandment:
"You shall love your neighbor as yourself."
This means to love one another as Jesus loved us—
and such love carries a cost.
Maybe death.
Probably death.
But Jesus tells us how he will welcome us
in the City of God:
"For I was hungry and you gave me food,
I was thirsty and you gave me something to drink,

I was a stranger and you welcomed me,
I was naked and you gave me clothing,
I was sick and you took care of me,
I was in prison and you visited me.
Truly, I tell you,
just as you did it to one of the least of these
who are members of my family,
you did it to me" (Matt. 25:35–36, 40).

Who are my brothers and sisters?
Who are the least in my community?
My sister is the hungry child born into poverty;
my brother is the sexually abused boy
or the gay man dying of AIDS
alone and deep in shame.
My sister is the recovering alcoholic
and the teenager destroyed by addiction to crack;
my brother is the unborn child.
My sister is the woman raped and beaten;
my brother is the criminal in prison;
my sister is the elderly woman alone and unloved.
My sisters and brothers are the millions

". . . to one of the least of these . . ." (MATT. 25:40)

who cannot find a job,
and those too hopeless
even to muster up the desire to look anymore.
These are our brothers and sisters.
Who will speak for them?

Who will speak if we don't,
who will speak if we don't,
who will speak so their voice will be heard,
*Oh, who will speak if we don't?**

And it doesn't end there.
My brothers and sisters are also the ones
we call "monsters,"
the ones who have committed the despicable:
those who have murdered,
those who have participated in genocide,
those who abduct our children,
those who have made choices
in defiance of the vision of God.
Yet redemption is for them as well.
Salvation knows no favorites.
This truth of the gospel
is hard for many of us to stomach,
but it is God's promise,

*"Who Will Speak?" refrain, by Marty Haugen, copyright © 1993 GIA Publications, Inc., 7404 South Mason Avenue, Chicago, IL 60638.

hope beyond our dreams.
We are loved and held in God's eye;
truly *nothing* can keep us from the love of God.

Thank God for the visionaries and the heroes,
because after they have traveled the river of hope,
the rest of us can follow.
Thank God for the visionaries and the heroes,
because their courage
allows transformation to take place.
Thank God for the visionaries and the heroes,
because they make us squirm,
they call us to speak
loudly and passionately,
they call us to speak
where it would be easier to be silent.
Thank God for the visionaries and the heroes,
because they call us to responsibility.
Thank God for the visionaries and the heroes,
because they put the poor,
the suffering,
and the lepers

right in our face
and force us to confront
our own poverty and sickness.
Thank God for the visionaries and the heroes,
because they call us beyond ourselves
to name possibilities in the midst of impossibility.
Thank God for the visionaries and the heroes,
because they break open the comfort
of silence and numbness
and encourage us to pierce
the deafness of the world.
Thank God for the many blessed people in my life,
truly visionaries and heroes for me.
Because of them
I seek to live more passionately
the way of Christ,
and because of them
I am a better Christian,
a minister of greater integrity,
and a more loving and human person.
For these people I will be always thankful.

Five

Everything Will Live Where the River Flows

Wherever the river goes,
every living creature that swarms will live,
and there will be very many fish,
once these waters reach there.
It will become fresh;
and everything will live where the river goes.

—EZEKIEL 47:9

THE COURAGE TO SPEAK
and to live what we believe
enables transformation to take place.
This is how hope is born.
It is work,
it is commitment,
it is hard!
We find it hard to believe
that our situation can change,
that a new way can be found.
In our deepest imagination
we find it difficult to conceive of ourselves
different from how we find ourselves today.
We cannot imagine healing.
We cannot perceive of ourselves forgiven
in the way that God continuously forgives us.

We find it hard to tolerate that God loves those
who commit the most hideous of acts;
it seems almost a dream that there really is a God
who loves us no matter what.
We find it almost impossible to believe
that we are worth the effort,
that salvation is possible.

Everything will live where the river flows... *

Yet, when we sail down the river of hope,
when we see the possibility at the end,
and when we look back to where we have been,
we can see the evidence of God's grace
and the reasons to be hopeful.
We can stand on the witness of the faith
of parents and grandparents, friends and heroes
who time and time again have proclaimed loudly
the news of the resurrection.

---

*"Everything Will Live," refrain, by David Haas, copyright © 1995 GIA Publications, Inc., 7404 South Mason Avenue, Chicago, IL 60638.

They have continued down the river of hope
over and over again.

Because of this wonderful gift handed on to us,
we can say that it is not foolishness to believe
that healing is possible,
that we *can* move
beyond hurt,
beyond pain,
beyond suffering,
beyond death.
It is not nonsense to believe
that wholeness can be restored to our families
and to our relationships.
It is not foolish to believe
that peace, justice, and freedom are possible.

Everything will live where the river flows...

It is not insane to believe
that the poor can find a home worthy of the name.
It is not foolish to believe

that war can be eliminated
as a solution for tension among nations.
It is not irrational to believe that one day,
as Martin Luther King dreamed,
character, not the color of one's skin,
will determine one's dignity.
It is not crazy to believe
that addiction to drugs and alcohol and crime
can be conquered among our young.
It is not foolish to believe
that we can stop hiding behind the myth
that capital punishment is justified
to punish those
who have committed heinous crimes.

Everything will live where the river flows...

It is not foolish to believe
that our theologians will be able to dream
beyond the oppression of silence and conformity.
It is not naive to believe *and* expect
that one day women will be ordained.

It not madness to believe
that the church of the baptized,
and *not* the institution of the power-hungry,
the frightened, the paranoid, and the rigid,
will help realize the city of God on this earth.

Everything will live where the river flows...

These are not thoughts of fools.
I have a friend who used to tease me
because I am a big fan of Broadway musicals,
and I like to watch
the grand old movie musicals on video.
He would say:
"People singing and dancing in the streets,
how crazy!
People don't do that in everyday life."
And then I would say,
"Yes, but wouldn't it be great if they did!"
And then I watch the news
and see that we *do* sing and dance:
the people sang and danced

when Nelson Mandela was freed from prison
in South Africa;
many of us were glued to our television sets
as we watched the liberated people of Haiti
singing and dancing in the streets.
But we have to remember
that they sang and danced
before their freedom and liberation were realized.
Their celebration was constant:
they *sang and danced themselves* into their new reality.
Their celebration was not
just a result of their healing;
it was also the cause and origin of their healing.
So can it be for us.
It is *not* foolishness.

Everything will live where the river flows . . .

One of my favorite stories in the gospels
is the story of the Transfiguration.
Jesus takes Peter, James, and John
up to the mountain

. . . he was transfigured before them . . .
(MATT. 17:2)

and shows them a wonderful vision:
Jesus, Moses, and Elijah dressed in dazzling white.
Peter then says,
"This is great!
Let's build a tent and stay here forever!"

But what does Jesus do?
He snaps his fingers, and everything disappears.
They had to go back down the mountain,
but they went back different than before.
After attending a wonderful conference
or after making a powerful retreat
or participating in a meaningful liturgy,
we will say:
"Well, now we have to go back to the real world."
This is where the problem lies.
We have it all backward.
We keep thinking
that the world we go back to is real,
and that what we have experienced is the illusion.
My friends, what is out there — that is false!
What we have experienced is real!
And our call is to announce and live the real truth.
The truth that we *say* we proclaim
at liturgy on Sunday is this:
"Everyone is welcome at this table,
regardless of your economic status,
regardless of your gender,

regardless of your political affiliation,
regardless of your race,
regardless of your sexual orientation — everyone."
What we believe about the Eucharist
and the wonderful galaxy of people
who make up the Body of Christ
is *the ultimate truth.*
This is the truth we need to invest in.
This is the truth that we need to proclaim.
This is the truth that we can believe in,
not the falseness of the everyday world.
It is possible,
and we celebrate it
when we worship in spirit and truth.

Everything will live where the river flows...

One of our great stumbling blocks
as we look down the river of hope
is that we doubt our own abilities,
our own giftedness, our own call by God.
We find it difficult to believe

that God would call *us*.
We often say: "Well, I'm not really worthy.
I mean,
if they really knew what kind of person I was,
well, you know.
I am not really that good of a person."
Once again, we have it all wrong:
worthiness is not the issue.
We have to realize that hope often springs forth
from the most unlikely and unpredictable places.
Once again, we have to look to the Scriptures
to see who God called:
Moses could not even speak well;
he had to have Aaron as his mouthpiece.
Yet he is the one
who led the people from bondage into freedom.
Jeremiah was too young,
David was too short,
Jonah had a fish fetish,
and Job was manic depressive.
All we know about Gideon
is that he was an absolute bore —

all he did is leave Bibles in hotel rooms.
And then look at Peter.
Peter of the Transfiguration story who didn't get it.
Peter in the boat with Jesus having a panic attack
because the storm was getting out of hand,
shaking and waking Jesus up saying:
"My God, we're going to die!"
Peter who has the need
not just to have his feet washed,
but his entire body, and Jesus says,
"Calm down, Peter, just the feet."
Peter who has delusions of being Errol Flynn
or Luke Skywalker,
who has to take out his sword at Jesus' arrest
and shouts out: "I will save you!"
and cuts off the soldier's ear,
and Jesus says: "Peter, chill out."
Peter who ultimately denies even knowing Jesus.
And yet this is the man we claim as our first pope.
This quivering bowl of jello is named "rock."
Our world and our church
are consumed and obsessed with perfection;

Peter would not pass
a Roman Congregation's inquiry.
God calls us —
with all of our imperfections,
with our sinfulness,
with our clutziness.
And it is in the manifestations of
clumsy, sinful, and broken human beings
that Christ is most present.
Look around you!
See the presence of Christ!
Welcome and reverence that presence
in the person beside you!
Don't look up to the heavens,
or into the waves of the sea,
or to the majesty of the mountaintop.
Rather, take a moment right now
to look into the eyes of the person next to you.
See Christ,
see the hope that is possible,
see courage and faith!
See the stories and struggles.

Everything will live where the river flows . . .

We have to continue to proclaim loudly
and remind ourselves that God is in charge.
God is the only one
who could have directed recent events.
Who would have thought
that rebel and prisoner Nelson Mandela
would become president of South Africa?
Who would have dreamed
that a poet, not a politician,
would become president of Czechoslovakia?

Who would have thought
that a banned union worker named Lech Walesa
would become president of Poland?
Who would have thought
that the Berlin Wall
would come down in our lifetime?
Who would have thought
that we would ever see Israel and Jordan
sign a peace agreement?

Certainly Sr. Helen Prejean
never would have imagined
that an initial gesture
to be a pen pal for a death row inmate
would result in an award-winning book and movie
that would touch people all over the world
and expose the sin of the death penalty.

Who would have believed
that an unassuming old man,
Pope John XXIII,
would call a council
that would set the church on its ear?
It is the river of hope
that keeps things alive and well!

Everything will live where the river flows . . .

There are a lot of nay-sayers in our church.
There are people who think Vatican II was a mistake,
and there are those in the institution
who want to take us backward.

They want to silence the visionaries and the heroes;
they want to stop the renewal.
Their tactics at times definitely slow reform:
by outlawing liturgical and highly regarded
biblical translations,
by squashing attempts to use inclusive language,
by trying to halt liturgical creativity,
and by enacting strategies to end discussions
about the role of women
and about women's ordination.
Many who are in "control" want to banish prophets
and to institute more rigid guidelines
for what we can believe and not believe.
They have chased many wonderful people,
many talented people, out of the church.
They would rid the church
of all who dream of a church
based on service and mission
so they can control things their way.

But they have forgotten an important thing:
that God is in charge!

You cannot control the spirit of God!
You and I have to stand tall
and proclaim loudly to the cynics and nay-sayers:
NO WAY!
I don't know about you,
but I am not going back.
I'm staying here in this church.
They're not going to find it easy to get rid of me.
I'm going to stay right in their face
and then say, Guess what?
I'm still here.
Why?
Because God is in charge.
And that river of life and hope
is too strong for anyone to stop it.

Everything will live where the river flows...

With eyes of hope, we can journey down the river.
We are all invited to go there.
If we sign on to the adventure,
we will see the wonderful good news made real—

that the resurrection is not fantasy!
Christ is not some imaginary superhero.
Hope is not naive optimism.
It is here, right now, all around us.

Everything will live where the river flows...

When hope becomes the banner
under which we live,
we know that God's vision is possible.
We can believe
that there really is a blessing awaiting our children.
We can face the poor,
the person with AIDS,
the suffering, the outcast,
and believe that God is for them
and that justice is not far away.
With this hope we can believe
that race, class, and gender
will not matter,
and that the ability to make war
and possess great wealth

will no longer be the measure of our security.
We will be able to build, envision, and dream
a new world.
Hope means believing and watching things change.
This is the kind of hope that leads to true faith,
a faith that takes us
to the edge of the cliff
of all that is secure and known,
and then leads us to take one more step.

Everything will live where the river flows . . .

It is difficult to believe that the reality changes,
because it seems as though
death, pain, and suffering
continue to flourish.
The challenge is to face
the reality and presence of suffering.
In Mark's Gospel right after Peter says to Jesus,
"You are the Messiah,"
Jesus responds with an amazing paradox
that is hard for us to swallow:

. . . those who trust in the Lord . . .
shall be like a tree planted by water,
sending out its roots by the stream. (JER. 17:7–8)

"The Son of Man must suffer much,
be rejected, . . . be killed."
We do not need to be alive for very long
to understand that suffering, pain, and death

are inescapable —
even though we spend so much of our lives
in denial and efforts to escape them.
Suffering is part and parcel of our living experience.
We often cry out in anguish
that we do not understand
why God allows bad things to happen.
I do not know why God
does not just wave a magic wand
to rid us of the terror that surrounds us.
But this much I do know:
This God loves us enough to become one with us,
to walk with us in the terror of life,
to feel the pain that we feel,
and to die on a cross.
My God does not find joy in war,
in AIDS or cancer,
in comas or HIV;
God does not revel in my hurt
and the demons that haunt my soul and psyche.
But God does offer me a way out
or, rather, a way *through* it all,

and keeps my suffering from turning into horror.
How?
By turning my pain into service,
by inviting me to transform my suffering
into sacrifice and dedication;
to transform my cynicism and hopelessness
into faith for the sake of another,
and by taking the many dyings in my life
and planting new seeds for others to live.
The resurrection does not promise
that suffering and pain will be abolished.
The promise is that death will not win,
it will not be the last word,
it will not be our destiny.

Whenever we feel frozen,
frustrated or discouraged,
whenever we feel helpless or hopeless,
we need to focus and have faith
that our situation is not as bad as it would seem.
Hope always begins in the midst of hopelessness.
It is about new possibilities;

it is to believe that we are not trapped
by the condition in which we find ourselves.
It means to live life with purpose and dedication,
dedication to what lies down at the end of the river,
the possibility of unimaginable quality and quantity,
that is, life and hope to the full.
Quite simply,
it is about investing the totality of our hope
in the victory of the paschal mystery:

> *Yet I believe beyond believing,*
> *that life can spring from death;*
> *that growth can flower from our grieving;*
> *that we can catch our breath*
> *and turn transfixed by faith.**

*"Each Winter As the Year Grows Older," stanza 4, by William and Annabeth Gay, copyright © 1971 United Church Press.

Wherever the river goes,
every living creature that swarms will live,
and there will be very many fish,
once these waters reach there.
It will become fresh;
and everything will live where the river goes.

—Ezekiel 47:9

crossroad